T0083559

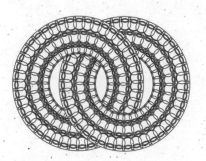

THE SNOW'S WIFE

THE

SNOW'S

WIFE

FRANNIE LINDSAY

CavanKerry
PRESS

CavanKerry Press Ltd.
Fort Lee, New Jersey
www.cavankerrypress.org

Publisher's Cataloging-In-Publication Data
(Prepared by The Donohue Group, Inc.)
Names: Lindsay, Frannie, author.
Title: The snow's wife / Frannie Lindsay.
Description: First Edition. | Fort Lee, New Jersey : CavanKerry Press, 2020.
Identifiers: ISBN 9781933880815
Subjects: LCSH: Lindsay, Frannie—Marriage—Poetry. | Husbands—Death—Poetry. |
    Grief—Poetry. | American poetry—21st century. | LCGFT: Poetry.
Classification: LCC PS3612.I533 S66 2020 | DDC 811/.6—dc23

Cover and interior text design by Ryan Scheife, Mayfly Design
First Edition 2020, Printed in the United States of America

CavanKerry Press is grateful for the support it receives from the New Jersey State Council on the Arts.

Also by Frannie Lindsay

Where She Always Was (2004)
Lamb (2006)
Mayweed (2009)
Our Vanishing (2014)
If Mercy (2016)

for Lizzie

CONTENTS

III

THE SNOW'S WIFE

Falcon

Your body lay alone with its readiness.
We shared our bright, harsh peace with the air
of the porch, the sun a gentle stranger.
The squirrel you once shooed from the feeder
snatched a white crust of your sourdough.

We laid our palms down
in your sternum's precipice. We rested our hands
in your silent, white hair, on your ears
and your white, unfeeling fingers. We dried the tear
that remained on your cheek.

We opened the drapes. We opened the cupboards.
There were your goblets, the rest of your whiskey.
Your pocked birthday spoon. Clean tea towels
folded, asleep. And your bathrobe, tall
on its hallway hook.

On the bedside table, water stood in its cup.
Your thirst had stopped. The Christmas cactus
put forth a blossom. Your King James Bible
perched on its chestnut stand like a falcon,
wings opened wide to Isaiah.

Once I watched a female peregrine
swoop on a field mouse. I watched some boys
swoop on a muddy red Frisbee. Their clean
hair glistened. In the white chapel, an amateur choir
fumbled an anthem's opening notes.

The peregrine came to rest on a birch tree's
scarred white arm. It shook with her sudden weight.
Some dry leaves fluttered with afterlife.

She came for her lonesome feast. Her labor
of snapping the still moist bones.

In the harsh and bright noon's peace,
she tore and ate.

I

God with us

you will know this child
by the heart it has pieced together—

sticks and a single tear of fire

before we were made

  ఔ

you will know this child
by all who claim

to have orphaned it

  ఔ

and by how it has never needed

toys of this earth

not a name
not a pony

Bead

I still have the shirt he wore to the doctor
the day she took both his hands
and looked into his milky eyes
and told him
as if it were some kind of blessing.

None of us cried, none of that—instead
we sat in an awkward huddle and skimmed
the scan report, all seven single-spaced pages
making no sense, especially to him,
who swore to God

that a life was a string of beads
made of single bright days,
and all you needed to do to be happy
was thread them, now and then hold your strand
up to whatever light there was, but always

keep a firm grip on the bead
you were passing your red string through
that very moment. Then go back
to your stringing, and go back
again, until they were gone.

Invitation

Go now to the silence. It has longed for you
as a mother longs for her ransomed child.

Go, and take off your shoes, your gloves,
weave from your shadow and ache

a rough blanket. Lie down. Your body
knows itself everywhere now,

just as a deep sky knows each river and cliff,
each still meadow lazily dotted with goats.

Take off your watch cap. Allow wind
to carry it off like a raveled nest

and mingle your hair with the grasses
winter has already burned away. Allow sleep.

Allow gratitude. Allow the essential and hesitant
leave-taking. Now may the soft-eyed wolves

approach with the same moon
tucked in their hearts and their hungers ordained.

Now like a sprig of thistles a schoolgirl picked,
may you be forgotten.

And your old name join its fellow rustlings,
and you always be loved.

Dying Boy

Instead you will be with
your owl collection
your brown and orange shirts
the paintings by your friend
but you ask me
in your milk voice still-here voice
can you have another hill of pillows
for your knees that have turned
already back into snow
and can I bring our wedding quilt
its squares of summer stories
and can I leave the light on
please

Elegy in October

Why not reunite at the library,
the afternoon aflutter
with children gathered close
to hear a story in a corner
festooned with their cutouts;
and college students slumped
across their carrels, pretending not to
check each other out? Aren't hormones
gorgeous? Don't you wish we could
still wear their great, embarrassing
corsages? Fall is wilting, agonal
and golden in the courtyard birch.
Come, and drape your shadow's
pilled, unsavable cardigan
across the wing chair I have nestled in
to riffle pages. Come while no one knows
I am expecting you. For I can't
stay long either.

Refuge

You didn't have your cane. The dark March wind
made you weak. You only had a little way to go.
You leaned against a stucco wall I saw once
in your travel books. You wanted aspirin.

Your scarf was much too tight. Your hat gone.
Something more was wrong. You'd lost
your wedding ring. I brought a cup of water
and two pills. I brought them through the snow.

I brought a cap that didn't fit. You should have been
deep in your shadow's boat, a little bit asleep,
a reed between your teeth. The snow, had it been kind,
would fall again like old magnolia petals

loosening all at once when it was time—
and go on falling, burying your boot tracks.

Prayer without a Voice

Beloved and exiled God be with us
now in the glare of our sickness
place on our brow a rag of sacrament
drenched with the tears of the damned
lift us into your black hammock's sway
remind us again that we can no longer
awaken even one star
and nothing but this
needs your breath

In November, Everything Departs

Behold the sunshine, draping
its already-weary cloak over the noontime
pond. Behold the peregrine's gaze, clear
of rumor. Behold the brambled railroad track
at the end of wander.

Behold the black dog
watchfully curled around the soupbone
she's worried down to its lifeless gleam.
Behold the plaid shroud
of her blanket.

I have been willing the finches to fall
silent and join the sullen
wet of the leaves. Willing my friends to keep
out of the way. Stars to keep out of the way
of the night clicking along

its rainy avenue. But behold, too,
the bosomy gloom of libraries. The lamps,
so earnest and adequate over the little desks.
I can bear to look as happiness fades
from its tedious season. I can endure

each vesper bell tonguing against
its brave lip; the thrill in words like *reckon*,
atone, and *widow*. How they are one another's
encrypted siblings. The things they know.
The things they harken.

To alienation

In your shadow's long April,
a grove of pale caretakers

In your banishment's fury,
a boy who will not turn away

In the choristers' voices,
barn light

In each jeweled ravage,
barn light

In the heart of your brother,
a hound who has limped over snows

On your mantle,
the vase of your last-born's breath

Widower, kneel
by the names of your darkly beloved,

for nothing utters them now
and the vespers are everywhere

And in the sea,
the thorned sea

Prayer for My Rapist

I hope he has learned
to slink unnoticed across the nights'
sad meadows, leaving the asters
alone in their clusters, evading
the blackberries' thorns. So much
running: from pillow-slam,
scream-and-I'll-kill-you, knife-
in-the-sock, from bureau shoved
in front of bathroom door. From
seven streaked Polaroids.

He has a silky scar
on the left just under one eye. He is
short. His hair is lush as a puppy's.
Touching him saves my life.
Remembering him saves my life.
Crouch him in any dark. Deprive him
of fingerprints. I will always be
wide awake although he is old,
a little less mad, cleaned up.
Something about the things

that a stare can't freeze, the squalid
rattle deep in the ribs. It is only
a cough. It is only a trapped wolf's fury.
It is the sum of his father's father's
despair, no more than that.
He has no shirt. He has no coat.
His shoes are torn. He is thirsty. His legs
are weak. He clatters and trips.
The soft grass offers him only
the might of her pity.

Cry

#BringBackOurGirls

Bring back our dresses untorn
bring wind for them
bring our barrettes
and the pretties we wanted
bring back our chalk
and the flies with no secrets
bring tear-splash
on kerchieves of mothers
bring solace for wailing
cover o cover our asking eyes
line up our shoes
keep sharp our pencils
and latched our boxes of paints
bring back our off-key hymns
bring back the cram of our knees
under outgrown desks
bring the cloudless skies of our boredom
bring back the whisperless waiting
the nudging of nothing
the knowing the flinch
against our against
bring back our lesson books
written in hurriedly
bring back the doorway's breeze
when we finished our learning
bring back our chatter
that weighed less than birdsong
bring back the cursive
we almost were good at
the grasses waving at no one
bring the tall of the trees of us

keep hot the schoolhouse embers
bring spears from the hearts
of startled gazelles
bring back the stars
with their dawn-time ferocity
bring back the masks of our
unsleeping faces

morning

for Denny

but then there is always
the square bed of sun
that the east-facing window delivers
in time for the dog to lie down
basking beneath the piano
in only herself

and there is the piano too
with its horselike kindheartedness
its sleek peace
and in the next room
which never has needed a door

the radio turned down low
by the lamp and the freesia
on the small dented table
speaking its terrible stories
that sound at this volume
like late summer insects signaling
their million-year-old acceptance
that this is the end of their lives

and there is always the woman
who hasn't been raped in over forty years
making her coffee her oatmeal making
the home that no one can ever
make for her

in the burning childhood house

I look to my mother my father
dead not yelling
and to my living sister
we are seated all polite as if on a Sunday

grandfather clock
cellos under the piano
melted ice in our four metal tumblers
there is nothing left to do

we are white-haired now and can't tell
precipice from gale
I get up to close the many windows
that need it

my footstep's clatter can't keep up
the flames unfurl their banners
like ladies who never liked children
finally tearing their dancing skirts off

here at the end of
the book I read only by flashlight
someone has left the cookies I made
so very long ago

on a plate I have never seen

Geoff

I like the man who rides the same bus
as I do, gets off one stop before me,
has silver hair, a downy black beard,
wears mostly jeans and a linen shirt. I like
his Birkenstocks, wire rims, and
frowsy eyebrows. I like the fatigue
around his mouth as if he's afraid
his daughter might have anorexia.
I like watching the things he is watching.
Women pushing along fold-up grocery carts,
almost spilling their boxes of cereal.
Signs for the same lost cat. I like his air
of dreamed-upness. I like kidnapping him,
eloping, having some children but first
a puppy, and lots of sex. I like the chitchat
we never stop or start, and his make-believe
name—*Geoff* spelled right, with a G—and
I like to cast off the gloom
of my lonesome truth, pay both
our fares, and take him home.

Impressionism

The minute I saw the man in the sky with his goat,
I wanted to marry him. So I asked the goat

for her acrobat-comrade's hand
in wedlock. She nodded. Some flowers

she had just started chewing
fluttered loose from her mouth. I did not

gather them up, for this
is the world, fraught now with metals and questions,

where bright colors once were friends
with everything—azaleas. A peacock's boastful display.

Vast, sunshiny baskets on heads. And I knew
if I married the man I would have to let the goat go.

II

August

How I have taken for granted

the galaxies of crickets

the black dog resting
her head on the ample moon

these nights
laying their calm blankets out

to forget me

Brushing the Horse

I am tired of praying for a world not ours
to break: the hushed hawk-sweep
blackly lifting two hundred schoolgirls
into the breathless Nigerian moonlight,
the fourteen-year-old who has murdered
his beautiful algebra teacher. For the soft-eyed
extinctions. We age in the glare
of the news. Give me instead
the floor of a barn in the gray of Heaven,
wet with the scuttle of hand-fed rabbits,
their twitch and trust. Give me
sparrows' wings scattering hay,
the gentle chill of the rafters,
the tumbled and redolent towels for carrying
peahens back to their safe, dim coops,
the hinges arthritic with rust;
a cracked bar of soap by the cold-water sink;
the sun going in like a wife who needs to
peel the potatoes; the last truck
gone for the day, a plaid shirt draped
on a gate; a broom whose bristles
flip like the hair of a girl who is ready
to go to the Friday dance at the grange.
Give me a roan mare's cheek;
the smell of apple, of patience.

Saturday

I thought I should never be happy again but here is the pond
that slakes the whole thirsty city.

Here are the long-necked trees leaning over
the water, all getting along with each other,

and here come two women in saris the color of peace
that could last a while,

and here comes the girl with pink flashing stars
on her shoes. I would not wish the sixth grade on anyone,

but the stones seem to like the sting of her feet. Here comes
the man who keeps falling headfirst

into all of the ashes of Lent. He is forgiven and seems startled
as if he is just now hearing a harpsichord.

I thought I should not be happy again, but I have a mother
who turned a hundred and twelve today.

She was never appalled enough, so I am inviting all of them
home for tea.

November on Fresh Pond

But most of all I have loved
afternoons the color of found pennies

and dogs at home in the worlds
of only their names

and the lonely
tall and at peace with their shadows

everything seems to be holding hands
although it is nothing perhaps

but the light with great care
joining together the proper ends of things

for in this deep moment there is almost
enough touch

and I have loved the sun lowering itself gingerly
into the smooth gray water

like an old woman sore from her long good day
taking a last quick swim

Angel

Even then she had to be fed by hand
her gray bowl on a stepstool

her kibble thinned
with room-temperature water then beaten
to mush

sometimes I stroked her throat
to help her swallow

the vet said it was nothing but
simple mechanics
getting the gruel to her stomach

she'd need six meals like that all her life
day after resolute day

sometimes she'd throw all of it up and
I'd have to start over

she would never weigh more
than the 45 pounds she brought with her

eight littermates having loped off to
glad solid lives Angel would never

have anything more than one
weary human who knelt deep in February

to slide the geranium-pink sweater over
her solemn head

she was wearing it still
penned in that small afternoon with

so many others

Farewell Blessing

Lord, receive the soul of this good dog
who comes to You in unmarred innocence;

may he now rest his chin against
Your knee's great ledge;

may he be met by friends remembered
and new friends;

may his leash be without end, his collar easy,
paws forever fleet;

may his panting remain close to those
alone at Sunday's dusk

so it may warm them by the flameless hearth
of his forbearing peace;

may he sleep within the perfect oval
of the moon's light on a window seat,

and each star know him by its light along
the pasture of his wintermost fur;

Lord, receive him, run to him
with the exuberance of little children;

then let him stay
exactly who he is—

his mystery, his everydayness.

To a Mourning Dove Rescued from the Curb

I saw you (will see you) zigzagging
skylessly along
gravity's lop-side stony side

your underneathness bloodied
and your feet like untied red strings

I folded you (will go on
folding you)
in a kindergarten-bright dishrag

and shoebox
with stars stabbed in the lid

o gray-feathered peacebringer
stashed among
the Wellies overcoats leashes

all the long and rustling night
while I dreamed I knew what to do

you fluffed for the expert warmth
you were going to need
to widow the sunrise

Goldfinch

You must have fallen asleep
in your yellow party dress,

but your eyes are the same
inlaid marcasite stolen from an old

pair of opera glasses,

and the black-lace edge of your wings
would look torn from a tired brassiere

were it not for the bright, bright
hollow of you,

how you fit in my hand
like a sacrament

as the chill breeze finds its way back
onto the sky more alone

than ever,
quick as a minus sign.

small remembrance

dog birthdays
tend to go off by their lonesome

pollen on dishes of water
notice or don't

Ox

She hears only the wind of their voices
but she knows they are lost
by the way the desert grasses tilt
toward the manger instead of the village,
and she has no way to rally herself
for the large, dour men
so she bristles, whips an imagined gnat
with her tail, has only
the whorls of her toneless horns and
her hooves' dull stones to defend
the cold little family huddled around
the lamp that keeps going out
while the alarming starlight stings her eyes
like a distant plea for rest,
and in the sweep of her breath's coarse robes
they come nearer, nearer,
laden with ominous gifts

The End of the Walk to Bethlehem

It has been days since we have slept
or spoken of the rumors fluttering
unchecked as moths among our lamps
while we rinsed the sheep
and latched them, damp still, in their pens
the dreary morning we set out,

and we want only to turn back,
and to believe again
in nothing, but we see the outline of
a stable, almost real, hunched
against the desert cold as if
unworthy of the star

that lights its roof, so we press on,
now stumbling, now holding one another
up, and draw as near the cradle as the ox
will let us, and set down at last
our gilded weariness.

The Arrival at the Manger of Those Who Mourn

The Infant will sleep through
the rustle of the cloaks, the nomads
shaking out their pebbly sandals
at the stable door, and through
the clop of camel hooves beneath
the shifting weight of gold and myrrh.
Even through the blare
and pageantry of approaching kings,
hushed now for Him
by common stars.

He stirs, instead,
a little bit toward sunrise for
the shambling guests
whose smudged and windburnt faces
He has always known
belong here: the indigent,
the shunned, the grieving
mother who can hear her stillborn's
milkless cry, sharp and new
as winter daylight.

the good world

but when I painted the deer
I didn't want to scare her

so I started with the leaves
her slow tongue curled around

then the nearby apples come loose
on their brittling stems

for her alone

I painted even the halfheartedness
of that red then

her eyes closing, leaving the sun
to tire by itself

as her lips rolled wetly across
their amiable consonant of eating

then I stopped
for it was her long day's end

but some apple still glistened

on the tip of my brush

III

Vesper

after Rilke
for my grief workshop students

When I am done with all this
living,

grant me
an earthenware dish

for the things
my fingers have brushed

as God passed by,
especially

that white hair, that flickering
eyelid, that lake water.

In the Before

Those mornings, just after the cancer
had stolen into your bones,

I walked the dog early, the weak moon
still out, coat over pajamas,

your woolen socks under my snow boots,
a half-awake grip on the leash,

no cars yet, nothing
to prove we were there, just an ephemeral

helix of pawprints and bootprints,
and when we came home to bed

your sleep drifted open for us
like the arched oak door

to St. James Church, where you hoped—
where I hoped—

you would be strong enough
to go back on Easter.

The Listening Room

I wish you would let me
wash your hair
comb your T-shirts
there is spaghetti
everywhere now
the sky is a mess with it
we have been cautioned
against looking up
the mourning doves can't find
the calls of their mates
through the tangle
your wheelchair is stuck on
a crooked rug at the end
of nothing but books
you are leaving your children
the goblets are singing
the shards of your little song
nothing stands under
the right shadow
I promised I would
call no one
when we got to this point
we have no more eye drops
your hearing aid picks up
the dark dark please
let me go
to the listening room
and pray for at least
your hair

Golgotha

for Holly Antolini

Then they came and cleansed you my love
with a separate sponge for each arm
each hand and its citizen fingers
each leg and each foot pale as magnolia
and swept a burst of holy wind through your hair
for ease of travel and then they anointed
one of your kerchieves with tap water
and made new your chest and belly
and blurred your sex
then they gathered
their competent shadows
and turned you
muscled with tender indifference
your boulder of pain
onto a kinder place and smoothed you
and pressed upon your tongue
a Eucharist of ice
and raised the blinds
on the wild and sleeping day

Benediction

Now may this remnant strand of you
tangle with the lichen in a barred owl's nest

Now may your glory of God
twine round the limbs of your lilac

and your Wellingtons lean in the doorway
like siblings many years distant

Now may the moonlight befriend
your gooseneck lamp and your hassock

Now may your fountain pen sip
from a sacred black

Now may your deathbed gather
all of the June nights' pollen

as you need no longer
discern your embers from starlight

scattered to usher you
home to the lie

Unction

At last you became less sick
skin feverless hummingbird pulse

as fewer visitors
laid their palms against your cheek

as your sleep turned back into
the Saturday weather of meadows

and your thirst a mountain brook's
bright March trickle

as the words you had loved
darted forth like the musicless gray

of moths over the evening wind

and your hands the caves
in which mine still burrowed

gave up the last of their comfort
and grew dim for the night

Louise

She was here—no she was
really here. She had taken her shoes off—
sat down at the foot of your bed, hand on
your peace-white hand—

her picnic basket and sleeveless blouse,
elbows flecked again with beach sand—
she could still bear
to look at food—

and the sun had come back
for her hair, and it filled your room—
a braid gone quiet. And you were the camera
she smiled for.

afterself

1
rose from the midst of us
Fig Newton T-shirt just washed
quilt still rumpled afterself still surrounded by the few
who could bear to look

placed his hands on our shoulders
the tops of our heads

2
we saw him into the hatch of the silver van
under the grown-up leaves reaching their shade over the street
like hands clasped as if in a ceremony
the stars weren't looking they already knew

the van floated away as it carried
the evening its pallbearer
no noise just deafening gentleness

3
stillness that opens each day like a pair of empty hands
like Christ's tomb like the word *widow*
and also *grace*

4
he still insisted he could bake pies have friends in for dinner write his sonnets
dress himself
all this to distract the bad cells exploding like mines
from his bones' war-lands

and his soul racing around in the dust
to get ready

5
the clamshell night–light outside the bedroom guiding his steps
to the bathroom as they grew slower
then only with help
then not at all

unplugged
put away

receiving the Host

bless this oatmeal
this ice cream
bless shakes these awful
jammed–with–calories
thick so you can swallow
thick so you can live
a little longer bless
vanilla just enough
to get the pills down
bless this little Ovaltine
mixed in bless every spoon
on which your lips
still close this straw
that bends so you can live
o bless this syringe this
single liquid
dose as needed
bless this
little longer

elegy against itself

hated the winter mornings sunless as bedpans
hated the unsugared tea of nightfall in January

hated the bedside evenings
the orchid-pink morphine lined up in its syringes
like nervous girls at a dance

hated reading aloud
hated my voice but the words forward-marched
day by dry-mouthed day

hated the lamp kept on and your lit sleep

hated the nonrefundable season tickets the memberships

the bursting compost the fruit flies
dog-paddling in dishwater

Margaret's vacuum cleaner
its every Thursday no-matter-whatness

now I box up the soapstone pepper mill
wrap the owl collection in undershirts

press orange dots on the paintings I want

make room on my shelves

leave your moccasins
on the rocking chair I won't go near

a clean white sock rolled into each
like a fist in a mouth

Clairvoyance

After the death nurse went home
we had nothing to do
but watch the gray balloons of you
rise away first one then another
then the vast flock of them
so we opened even more windows
wanting everyone on the streets of the world
to know that this was
a joyful day among days
that you were sweeping across the morning
your prescient approving winds

The Cremation

I didn't wear black
to your burning
instead I wore
a pollen-green dress

didn't cry just read
the short prayer
I had jotted down
on the way

then laid my hands
on the place
on the box
where your face was

God said
my hands should be
where the box
said Head

and I asked
did He want me
before it was taken
to kiss the cardboard

A Welcome

When I am finished living,
give me a minute
to fill the bird feeder,
tend to the geraniums, rinse
the goblets, and set a plate
of cooling ginger cookies out,
and raspberries, and dark
Chilean chocolate.
Grant my wrist a final pivot
to uncork the good wine—
it should breathe awhile.
Then invite the wind's light in
to bathe my shoulder blades'
ridged dunes. Dress me
in the same bright skirt I wore
the night the cold rain tinseled
the pear tree's blossoms.
Fetch my wide, appalling hat.
My tango shoes. Help me
back to bed. Spread larkspur
in the vase where water
waits for them. Then leave
the faucet to its drip,
the stairs their creak. Imagine
any music.

Clear Summer Night

His clocks get put away. His dinner plates
packed in a friend's car for the Goodwill.
The crockery, no longer argued over, mum
in all its cabinet-dark. The pepper grinder
filled with bitter gravel. The wedding photos
boxed beside the Christmas ornaments,
their childhood lint. Arrangements made
for hauling off the wheelchair. He stayed
until a voice he knew he'd know
said he could stay no more. Then
he set forth simply, keys he never copied
stashed between his philodendron
and his books. His life was such
a raucous, happy tenant. Now his body
shines with vacancy: shades raised,
mail brought in, leftovers
tossed out. The exhausted kin go home
on flat, safe turnpikes. The moon is new.

The Rabbits of Upland Road

You are going to lose everything.
The funeral home will show up to gather
your father beneath a velvet shroud.
The red potatoes will sprout in their basket
inside the window. Someone will wash
and fold the bedding and give it away.
The neighbors' visits will stop.
The art will assess at barely a fraction,
and then you will run out of
boxes. The plants will wither. No one
will want the rare books. In time,
your handwriting, too, will tie itself
into mad tangles. You will never
be granted the mercy you pled for.
Your hoarse voice will startle you.
But look: two brown rabbits
have popped naïvely out from behind
the lilacs. In their lovely identical eyes
rests the gem of everyday trust. It needs
no faceting. Then the evening blinks although
it is nowhere near dark, and leaves you
alone with just enough thanks
to tear off one more rag.

Harpsichord

Finally we can close our Bibles
and our Books of Common Prayer,

promise everyone
a copy of the poem not finished yet.

We can empty both the vases of their lilacs.
Their soot-gray blooms lie crumbled

like fine insects on the tablecloth,
mute with its own private flowers.

We can fold the laundered shirts—
may they drape other shoulders smartly.

Finally we can pour out the unwanted soups,
examine each small apple in the crisper.

We can gather up the dumb and orphaned
bottles: morphine, haloperidol, neurontin.

The name on all of them
is no one's. They have no more

to ease. Pain stays where it is, but canceled.
Agitation, canceled.

The harpsichord looks startled
in the floor lamp's wing.

A wooden box of stamps with old cathedrals,
ticket stubs. A sixpence.

Finally on this broad new evening
we can open every door and window.

We can put more birdseed out.
The same marsh wrens will go on visiting.

After

No one died in your bed.
It is clean today as a plot
of daylight. The sheets
are new, the pillows nestled

like well-nourished children.
The packets of square blue swabs
for your lips, the folded diapers,
the delicate syringes: these

were props. Someone prays
as the wind grabs bone specks
away from her palms. The wind
has other blowing to do.

Someone cries, and the months
don't care. Someone tends
the plants and they bloom.
As if informed, the mail

stops. Then God appears
as a story, or as the breeze
where a story belongs:
you died

in your bed. We came.
We held your face. Summer
came too. We had to
allow her in.

listening elegy

at last you sit up in that weedy meadow
where you have gone

to tell me

you never wanted
the overcast tea that was not going to
make you stronger

never wanted your hair swept back

never the benzos the liniments

or friends whose names had come
to mean nothing
hunched late over takeout

never the window
open or shut

never the St. Francis prayer
or your lips swabbed

never wanted a fresh T-shirt
or the dog

never wanted your shadow's company
or gravity
or swift deliverance—

Andante

When I start to believe you are gone,
I put on the Beethoven String Quartets
you left me and 132's slow movement
folds me into a long and leafless evening,
and I place my hands deep
in your moccasins, which I have not
moved from the rocker's seat
and I wear them that way for a minute,
ridiculous mittens, then put them
back, nestle them close as veterans
sharing identical scars, and with the heel
of my palm, nudge the stuck bay window
and behold the courtyard maple's shy motion
and the limbs that are sick
with black spots, and behold
the inadvertent power of clouds, how
they break from their shapes that mean
nothing, not peasants haggling, not lions
or a brideless wedding procession, and
disperse to the place that no one
need ever remember.

Lullaby One Year Later

The things your children gave away
have been given away
again. A child practices her little cello
to your rosewood metronome.
Your schoolhouse clock now chimes
its quarter hours from a farmhouse kitchen.
Your ten-speed leans, unlocked, against
a shadeless chain link.

Some of your ashes
rest in a thrift shop urn beside
the piano, the others in the stony ground
of Maine. When I play the music
that you loved—*still* love—

I ask the notes for nothing.
Instead, I ask the close-by chips
of tumbled bone to gather themselves up,
put on your flannel shirt and out-of-fashion
chinos, your lamb's-wool slippers;
to nestle your hearing aids
deep in their caves of cartilage;

and when you are thus assembled
and can stay a moment,
to come sit in the rocking chair, and fall asleep,
for the phrase I labored over
has grown easy, and the same bay window
opens onto summer. Fall back to sleep
living, listening.

AFTERWORD

February 6 a.m.

If you wake
because the falling snow
is finally beginning
to sound like harpsichord music—

each string so exactly wound
the moon needs to practice somewhere else
before shining upon it,

and the painstaking rosewood scrollwork,
and the tense buds of anemone inlay,
and the solemn, confident legs—

remember how much
he wanted to leave you
the one he built.

Even the chosen sunrise
has taken years
to get this good.

ACKNOWLEDGMENTS

The following poems have appeared in these journals:

The Adroit Journal: "Andante"
American Journal of Poetry: "afterself," "Benediction"
Field: "August," "Unction"
The Missouri Review: "In November, Everything Departs"
Pensive Journal: "Clear Summer Night," "The End of the Walk to
   Bethlehem," "February 6 a.m.," "morning"
Peripheries: "Falcon"
Plume: "Angel," "Brushing the Horse," "Clairvoyance," "Cry," "Dying
   Boy," "Farewell Blessing," "Golgotha," "Harpsichord," "Invitation,"
   "The Listening Room," "November on Fresh Pond," "Ox," "Prayer
   without a Voice," "receiving the Host," "Saturday" (previously titled
   "The Pond"), "To a Mourning Dove Rescued from the Curb"
Plume Anthology 6: "the good world"
Poet Lore: "Refuge," "In the Before"
Salamander: "Louise"
Under a Warm Green Linden: "After," "Bead," "elegy against itself," "Prayer
   for My Rapist," "The Rabbits of Upland Road"
The Yale Review: "Elegy in October"

Heartfelt thanks are due as well to Anna Warrock, Julia Thacker, and
Robert Carr for their tireless guidance along the way toward many of
these poems' completion.

CAVANKERRY'S MISSION

CavanKerry is committed to expanding the reach of poetry and other fine literature to a general readership by publishing works that explore the emotional and psychological landscapes of everyday life and relationships.

OTHER BOOKS IN THE
NOTABLE VOICES SERIES

The Snow's Wife has been set in Bembo, created by the British branch of the Monotype Corporation in 1928–1929. It is based on a design cut around 1495 by Francesco Griffo for Venetian printer Aldus Manutius. Bembo is named for Manutius's first publication with it, a small 1496 book by the poet and cleric Pietro Bembo.